DRINKING · GAMES

Published by Crazy Coyote Games, PO Box 12 Diss, IT22 1YA.

ISBN 1-904139-98-1

Printed in Singapore

crazy
coyote
games

INTRODUCTION

Contained within this book are the rules to 50 all-time great drinking games. They can be played either at home or in the pub - all you need is a sense of fun and a full glass.

FORFEITS

It is in the nature of drinking games that a forfeit has to be paid by any player who fails to perform the task in hand satisfactorily. Inevitably, the forfeit is to take another drink, which makes the player's task that little bit more difficult in the next round. We strongly recommend that a non-alcoholic beverage is consumed as a forfeit. It is up to the players to agree the forfeits beforehand and to ensure that they are met. Drinking forfeits are measured as fingers of drink so that you line your fingers up against the liquid in your glass and drink to the bottom of one, two or three fingers.

MASTER OF CEREMONIES

It is most important that a Master of Ceremonies be appointed either for the whole evening or a different Master of Ceremonies before each game. It is imperative that the Master of Ceremonies does not drink any alcohol in order to fully carry out his or her responsibilities. They must monitor alcohol intake of all players, and they must ensure that no one drinking alcoholic beverages operates an automobile. The MC's responsibilities are wide ranging: they must adjudicate on any disputes, and make sure that the rules are abided by and that everyone gets a taxi home, or a ride home with someone sober.

The other players must address the MC as "Sir" or "Madam" throughout the game and must always request permission to speak to them. Any other form of address or, indeed, show of disrespect, renders the offending player liable to pay a forfeit.

The MC has the right to impose forfeits at any time, on any player, utterly at his own discretion and without the need of explanation. In fact he can be as biased and as prejudiced as he pleases! He should be helped in this task by a Chief Sneak.

The coveted position of Chief Sneak is awarded to the player who "sneaks" most often on his fellow players. He should report to the Master of Ceremonies any cheating, general bad behaviour and, most particularly, any "undue spillage" of a drink.

Players might like to implement the practice of having Half Hour Hands. For half hour periods, players are obliged to drink their drink using one particular hand. Thus they must take all drinks with their right hand from on the hour to 29 minutes past the hour and with their left hand from half past the hour to 1 minute before the next hour. Half Hour Hands can last for as many hours as the MC orders. Again the Chief Sneak can help in reporting any mistakes.

Please read the warnings at the back of this book before playing any of these drinking games. Failure to do so may result in serious injury or death.

We seriously recommend that you play these games with non-alcoholic beverages.

ESTABLISHED
SO LONG
AGO WE'VE
FORGOTTEN
WHEN

AVIATORS

K Mulhearn

AVIATORS

This is a game to be played in a house with a large number of rooms, or alternatively, on a pub crawl. Players form a large conga line and the leader is the "pilot". The conga flight takes it from room to room (or pub to pub) and each room visited is another country on their tour. Everybody has to take a drink which is the native tipple for that country (Guinness for Ireland, Pernod for France). The conga line then wends its way onto the next destination.

The pilot has responsibility for negotiating any turbulence, crash landings or air sickness amongst the passengers!

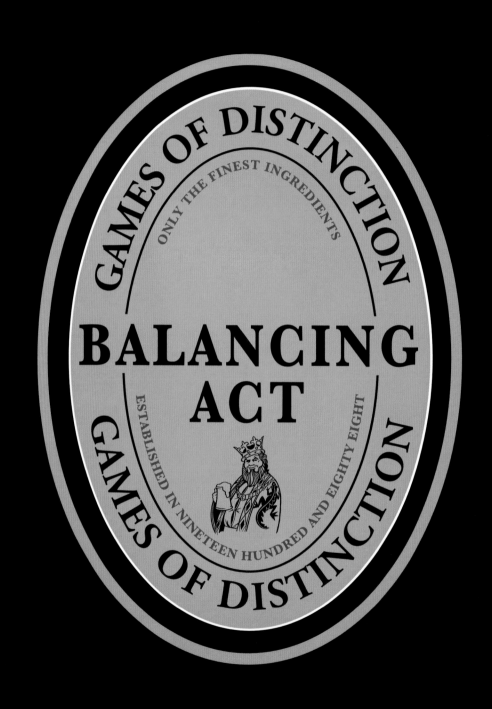

BALANCING ACT

EQUIPMENT: TWO CANS OF DRINK PER PLAYER

Draw a line on the floor to mark the starting point. Players take it in turn to stand behind the line with an unopened can of drink in each hand. They should rest each can on the floor, in front of the line, and then take steps forwards with the cans whilst their feet remain behind the line. The idea is to move one can at a time, gradually edging each one further forward. When a player has reached as far as they can, they must leave their can there. Then all they have to do is stand up again - without touching the floor! Thus you have to work your way back with both hands gripping the one can.

The player who places their can furthest away is the winner. Any player who touches the floor has to pay a drinking penalty.

WORLD'S FINEST

Beer
Hunter

PRIZE WINNER PARIS 1867
EDINBURGH 1888 CAMBRIDGE 1921

DRINKING GAMES

Beer Hunter

EQUIPMENT: A FULL CAN OF BEER FOR EACH PLAYER

One of the cans is given a vigorous shaking so that the contents will be well and truly lively! The cans are then mixed and swapped about so that the shaken can is lost among the others. Alternatively, they could be placed in a bag. One by one, players select a can and open it six inches from their face, with the can pointing towards them.

Some unlucky soul will have to suffer the humiliation of a can of beer exploding in their face!

BLIND
MAN'S BLUFF

ONLY  HOPS

FINEST
QUALITY

K Smith

ESTD 1988

BLIND MAN'S BLUFF

EQUIPMENT: TWO BLINDFOLDS

Players split into two teams. At one end of the room is a table with a drink for each team member on it.

The first player in each team is blindfolded, turned round ten times and then has to try and negotiate their way to the table to down their drink. Once they have done this, they must return to their team and hand the blindfold over to the next player.

Teams members are allowed to shout out directions. The losing team must buy the winners a drink.

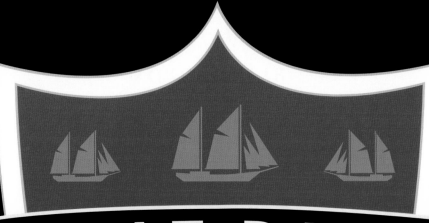

BOAT RACE

"only the finest ingredients"

BOAT RACE

Players need to form two teams. Each team stands in a line facing the other and every team member should have a full drink.

On the word "Go!", the first player in each team must down their drink and put their empty glass on their head. This is the signal for the next team member to start drinking.

The winning team is the one which finishes first and it is customary for the losing team to buy the victors their next drink!

BULLSEYE

EQUIPMENT: A GOLF BALL

This is a variation on "tag". Play starts when a player succeeds in dropping a golf ball into someone else's drink without them noticing. That player is now "It".

Once they have finished their drink they can retrieve the ball and use it to get their own back - at an opportune moment, of course. Players with a full drink are the most obvious targets!

If a player is spotted dropping the ball in by another player they must drink a four finger forfeit. If the ball bounces off the table or misses its target completely, then the player has to finish their drink as a penalty.

This game can be played with a coin instead of a golf ball for a subtler version.

This is the famous Bunnies Game. We know of no game produced which cost so much to manufacture. Our traditional skills and dedication make a game unequaled in the history of the world.

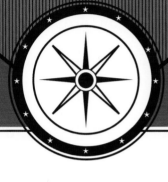

GENUINE

GENUINE

Estd   1988

Bunnies®

KING OF GAMES

Produced by traditional methods and only the finest ingredients

Bunnies ®

KING OF GAMES

The starter points their two index fingers at another player, thereby nominating them as the BUNNY. The BUNNY must respond immediately, by putting their thumbs to their temples and waggling their bunny ears; at the same time, repeating "Bunny, Bunny, Bunny...". The player on the BUNNY'S left must raise and waggle their right ear only, and the player on the BUNNY'S right must waggle their left ear only. Waggling must continue until another BUNNY is selected.

The BUNNY passes the go to someone else by removing their hands from their head and pointing their two index fingers at another player, who (along with those on either side) must start waggling ears appropriately.

BUNNIES may fake passing the go by pointing at another player with thumbs still firmly pressed to their temple - this is a False Pass. BUT, if the person pointed at foolishly starts behaving like a BUNNY, they pay a major drinking forfeit; those on either side, a minor forfeit.

"THE FAMOUS
BURNING BRIDGE"

BURNING

ESTD   1988

BRIDGES

3.5%

SERVE COOL

POUR RAPIDLY INTO

THE MIDDLE OF THE GLASS

BURNING BRIDGES

EQUIPMENT: TISSUE PAPER, ELASTIC BAND, A COIN AND A FULL PINT

Secure the paper on top of the pint using the elastic band. Alternatively you could just wet the edge of the paper slightly and place it over so that it sticks to the rim. A coin is placed in the centre of the paper. Players now take turns to burn holes in the tissue using a lighted cigarette. The loser is whoever causes the coin to fall through into the pint.

It is a question of how near the coin you dare go: the closer you are, the more difficult you make it for the next person!

The loser has to drink the ash-infested pint.

CAPTAIN BLUFF

OBJECTIVE: TO AVOID GETTING INTO A TANGLE!

The nominated player starts by saying "CAPTAIN BLUFF TAKES HIS FIRST DRINK OF THE EVENING". On saying this the player picks up their drink with thumb and ONE finger, takes ONE sip, puts it down tapping it ONCE on the table, taps their right shoulder with ONE finger on their left hand, taps their left shoulder with ONE finger on their right hand, taps their right shoulder with ONE finger on their right hand, and finally taps their left shoulder with ONE finger on their left hand. Once all players have succeeded in doing this, they move on to Captain Bluff's second drink of the evening, using TWO of everything, and then his third drink using THREE of everything, and so on. ANY mistake at all results in that player having to pay a drinking forfeit, and then trying again!

Cereal Madness®

EL
JUEGO
MAS
FINO

ESTD 1988

ADULT DRINKING GAME

Cereal Madness®

EQUIPMENT: AN EMPTY CEREAL BOX / SCISSORS

The box is placed on the floor and players take it in turns to pick up the box using only their mouths. No part of the body must touch the floor, except of course your feet!

Each player is given three attempts. If they touch the floor, fall over or have to stand up again, their go is over and they have to pay a drinking fine. If a player has still not succeeded after three attempts then they are disqualified.

Once everyone has had their go, an inch is cut from the top of the box, and the next round begins. The box gets smaller each round until only one player remains - the winner!

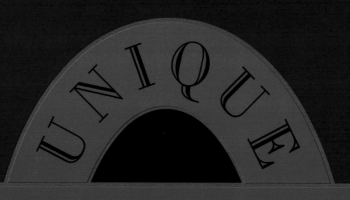

UNIQUE

CHAIN REACTION

TRADE
MARK

FULL FLAVOUR

CHAIN REACTION

Players need to be sitting in a circle or in a line against the bar. Players place both hands on the table or bar in front of them, crossing each hand with the player either side. Thus your left hand should be in front of the person on your left and their right hand should be in front of you; your right hand should be in front of the person on your right and their left hand should be in front of you. Try it - it's really quite simple! Someone starts by slapping one of their hands on the table. This should be followed by the next hand on the table and then the next etc. going round in order. This bit is more difficult then it sounds, especially when things inevitably speed up! The owner of any hand that does not slap when required has to take a drink, as does any nervous hand that slaps out of turn.

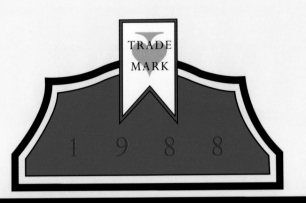

CHASE THE ACE

CHASE THE ACE

EQUIPMENT: PACK OF CARDS

Each player is dealt one card, face down on the table. Players take turns to look at their card and decide whether to swop it with the person on their left or keep it. The loser is whoever is left with the lowest card at the end and they have to pay a drinking forfeit.

If you elect to swop then you HAVE to keep the card passed to you. If a player holds a King (which is unbeatable) he can refuse to swop.

Aces tend to get passed round the table with alarming speed ending up with the poor dealer, so it is only fair that players should take turns at dealing.

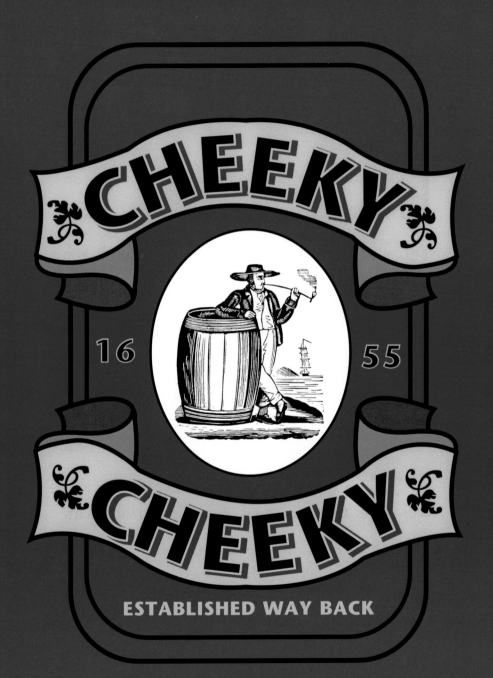

CHEEKY

16 55

CHEEKY

ESTABLISHED WAY BACK

CHEEKY CHEEKY

This game needs to include a "victim" player, someone who has never played before.

Players stand in a circle and the M.C. calls out orders. For example, "Touch the nose of the person on your left with your right hand", everyone does so, saying "nosey, nosey". This may be followed by cheeks, forehead etc.

What the victim is unaware of, is that the person next to them has dabbed their finger in an ashtray each time. They will be unable to understand the hilarity which everyone else seems to be suffering from as their face becomes increasingly blackened. Eventually take pity and reveal a mirror!

CLAPPING GAME

A PREMIUM GAME MADE TO THE HIGHEST STANDARDS. UNSPOILT BY DECADES OF PROGRESS.

CLAPPING GAME

Players sit round a table with their hands flat on the table top. The person who starts decides the direction of play and slaps their hands down on the table, one at a time. The next player follows immediately and play continues round the table. The following variations can be introduced at any time:

a double slap changes direction of play

a triple slap means slap alternate hands only

a quadruple slap means everyone has to take a drink. Inevitably, the speed of play increases. Any hesitation or mistakes incur fines!

OUR FOUNDER COMMANDER WILBURN

COMMANDER

To be played at

room

temperature

SINCE 1988

COMMANDER

Simon Says… for grown ups! A player is selected to be the Commander. Every time they give a command preceded by the word "Commander", the other players must perform it. If they give a command without the prefix "Commander", then players should NOT perform the deed and indeed anyone doing so is fined.

Specific commands which should be introduced are:

"Biblibobs" - wave the fingers of both hands up and down quickly.

"High" - hands raised up. Thus "Biblibobs high" would be raise hands up AND wave fingers.

"Very high" - stand and put hands in the air.

"Even higher" - stand on chair with hands raised.

These should be interspersed with "Low", "Very low" etc. Commands should be given at a rapid pace just to thoroughly confuse players!

estd 1988

DIRECTIONS

 THE FINGER POINTING IS A
REGISTERED TRADEMARK
OF THE DIRECTIONS BREWING CO.

PREMIUM GAME

LONDON ENGLAND

DIRECTIONS

Player one starts by determining the direction of play. If they place their right hand on the left part of their chest then play goes left, if they place the left hand on the right part of their chest then play goes right. The next player takes up the challenge and can either go in the same direction or change direction.

Sounds simple? As the game progresses however, concentration is definitely called for.

The FIFTH person must determine the direction by placing both hands on top of each other, and it is the fingers of the top hand which determine the direction. If they point right, play goes right; if left, left.

An additional rule applies to the TENTH player who simply points at any other player and the game starts again from that new point.

As usual, hesitation and errors attract drinking fines.

DROP DEAD

EQUIPMENT: 5 DICE

OBJECTIVE: TO TRY AND SURVIVE LONGEST

AND ACHIEVE THE HIGHEST SCORE!

Players take turns throwing the five dice, trying to get the highest score possible. If anything other than a 2 or 5 is thrown, the total spot value thrown is scored, the player takes a drink and throws again with all five dice.

If a 2 and/or 5 is thrown, the player scores nothing for that throw and the dice which showed the 2 or 5 are excluded from their next throw. This time, all the players watching take a drink!

Play continues until the player's last dice shows a 2 or 5. They are then said to have "DROPPED DEAD" and this point should be reinforced by a rousing chorus from the other players. Everyone takes a drink. The score is totalled and play passes to the next person. The winner is the player with the highest score at the end.

Fingers & toes

PLAY AT ROOM TEMPERATURE

— *1988* —

Fingers & toes

EQUIPMENT: TWO MATCHBOXES
AIM: TO FLICK YOUR MATCHBOX
INTO YOUR PARTNER'S GLASS

Two players sit on chairs opposite each other. Each has a glass on their chair resting between their thighs. The players get a matchbox and, using their forefingers as pivots, rest the box between their thumbs. They must now take turns to flick the box into the other's glass. Each time you succeed your opponent has to drink two fingers but scores are cumulative so that if they answer by flicking their matchbox into your glass, you now have to drink four fingers. The forfeit is only actually paid when someone misses, so tension mounts as the game proceeds.

A GREAT

A FINE

ESTD
1988

-FIZZ·BUZZ-

GAMES

DRINKING GAME

-FIZZ-BUZZ-

A QUICK-FIRE COUNTING GAME!

No drinking game compendium would be complete without this gem. Players sit in a circle and play goes round clockwise with players calling out "one", "two", "three" in order. When the number 5 is reached, or any multiple of 5, or indeed any number containing the digit 5, the player must say, "BUZZ" instead. Counting then continues round the circle. Once players are adept at this a new rule should be introduced: the digit 7 or any multiple of 7 must be replaced by the word "FIZZ". Thus play would go "3, 4, BUZZ, 6, FIZZ". It gets increasingly more difficult! Should you reach the dizzying heights of 57, this of course would be "FIZZ,BUZZ".

Anyone who gets it wrong is out - and has to take a drink. Undue hesitation should likewise be punished. The winner is the last remaining player, who is declared to be a mathematical genius.

4
JACKS
1 9 8 8

FOUR JACKS

EQUIPMENT: A PACK OF CARDS

This is a simple warm-up game. A pack of cards are shuffled and the dealer deals out the cards, one to each player, in full view of everyone. The player who is dealt the first Jack has to nominate a long drink.

The player who receives the second Jack names a chaser. The third Jack means the player has to pay for the drinks.

Whoever receives the fourth Jack has to drink them!

ADULT DRINKING GAME

FROGS

PREMIUM

 ESTABLISHED 1988

FROGS

Player one starts by saying "one frog, two eyes, four legs, plops into the pond".

The second player takes up the challenge by saying "Two frogs, four eyes, eight legs, plop, plop into the pond".

Play continues round the table.

Undue hesitation should be fined, as, of course, should any mathematical errors or mutant frogs.

This is not as easy as it sounds - particularly if played late in the evening.

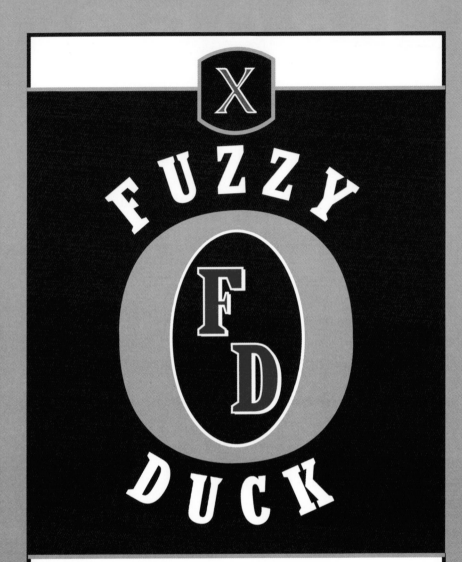

estd 1988

FUZZY DUCK

A TONGUE TWISTING, CONCENTRATION GAME!

One player starts by saying "FUZZY DUCK" and play passes to their left. The next player can either say "FUZZY DUCK" (in which case play passes to their left) or "DOES HE?" in which case a) play reverses direction and b) the player on the right says "DUCKY FUZZ".

Whenever play is moving in a clockwise direction, players should say "FUZZY DUCK", and when play moves in an anti-clockwise direction say "DUCKY FUZZ". Any player can reverse direction with "DOES HE?" at any time.

Any player speaking out of turn, or saying the wrong thing, pays a minor drinking forfeit. Any player asking a grossly indecent question has to pay a major drinking forfeit or choose a forfeit card.

Giraffe

ADULT
DRINKING
GAMES

TRADE MARK

SERVE
IN A TALL
GLASS

Giraffe

EQUIPMENT: AN EMPTY MATCHBOX

An empty matchbox cover is placed on the floor. Players take it in turns to kneel down on their hands and knees and try and pick up the box with their nose.

Anyone who falls flat on their face has to drink three fingers and tries again. If they fail on their second attempt they are out of the game.

In succeeding rounds, the box is moved further away. The winner is whoever succeeds in lifting the box from the furthest distance.

TRADE MARK

HARRY

ESTABLISHED
IN 1988

HARRY

Player one looks at another player and says "Harry?". That player must respond by saying "Yes Harry?", to which the first player responds by concluding "Tell Harry".

Now it is the other player's turn to say to a third player "Harry?" who should respond "Yes, Harry?" back to the second player, who does the same back to the first player. The games moves round the circle, with the question "Yes, Harry?" always being passed back to the first player.

If a player makes a mistake then they become "Harry one spot".

It gets increasingly difficult as the game speeds up. An alternative version is to play with the name Bruce for each boy playing and Sheila for each girl. Play must be conducted in an Australian accent.

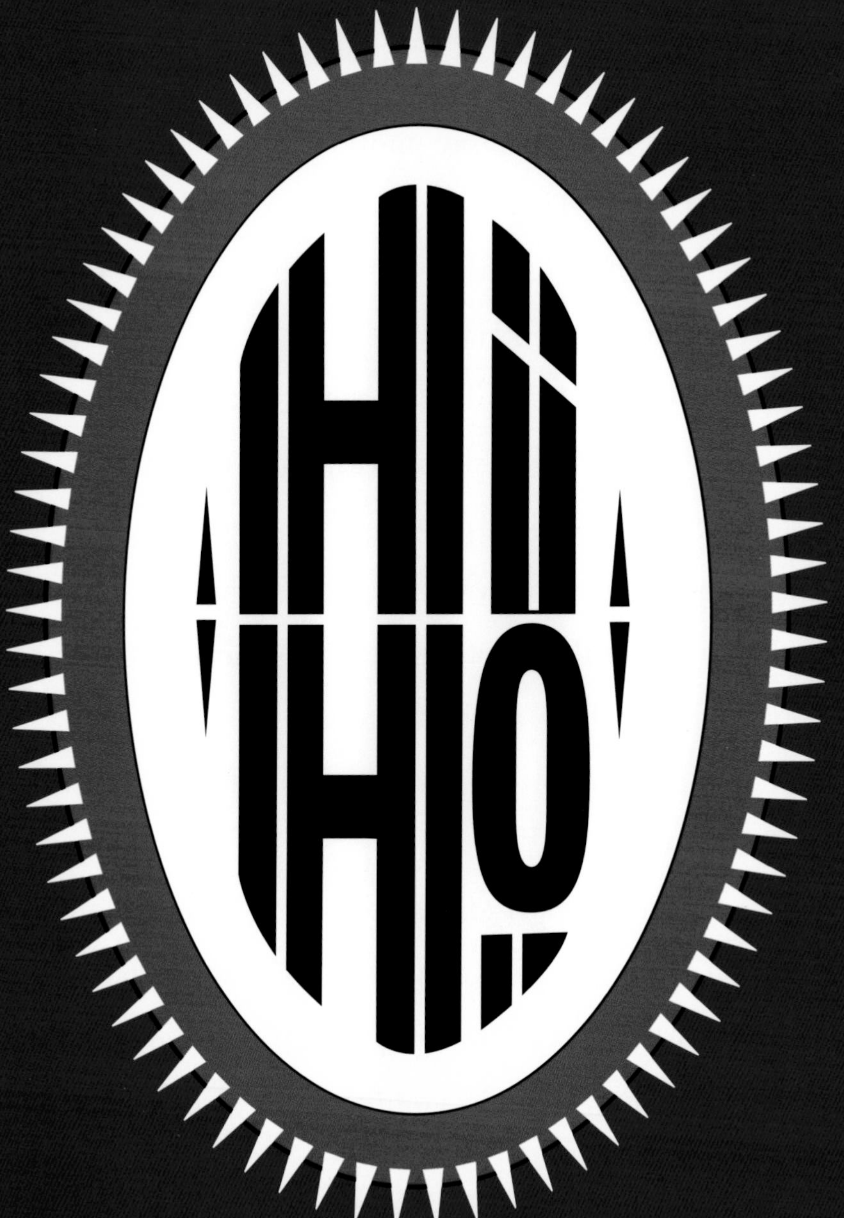

E veryone must know the words of the tune:
"Hi ho, hi ho, it's off to work we go,

with a shovel and a pick and a walking stick,

hi ho, hi ho, hi ho, hi ho, hi ho, it's off to work…"

The players sit round a table, each holding a bottle or can in each hand. They start singing and each time they have sung two words they pass the bottles to the person on their right, who also passes their bottles to the person on their right, and so on.

When you get to the line which goes "with a shovel and a pick", instead of passing the bottles on, you move the bottles to your right and then back again. You do this after every two words, so a total of five times. After "walking stick", you release the bottles to the person on your right and the song continues.

Chaos will probably ensue, depending at which point in the evening this game is played. Fines should be awarded liberally.

WORLD'S BEST

ADULT

DRINKING

GAMES

Ibble Dibble

WORLD'S BEST

ADULT

DRINKING

GAMES

Ibble Dibble

EQUIPMENT: A CORK BLACKENED IN A FLAME OR A PEN.

Players are numbered IBBLE DIBBLE 1, IBBLE DIBBLE 2, etc. going round the table. Number 1 starts the game by passing the "go" to any other player; they could say "IBBLE DIBBLE NUMBER 1 WITH NO DOBBLES, TO IBBLE DIBBLE NUMBER 6 (for example) WITH NO DOBBLES" and point to number 6. Number 6 then continues by passing the go to another IBBLE DIBBLE, and so on. This would be easy except for DOBBLES.

If a player makes a mistake and says something nonsensical, the cork is used to make a mark (a DOBBLE) on their face. If this happens to player number 4 for instance, they become IBBLE DIBBLE NUMBER 4 WITH 1 DOBBLE, and so on.

If a player points at the wrong player, becomes tongue tied, or uses the wrong number of DOBBLES, they must pay a drinking forfeit.

19 88

IN ORDER

Drinking Game
10% alc.

IN ORDER
OUT OF
ORDER

IN ORDER

This is an on-going game which anyone can start up at any point in the evening. It is best to try and catch people unawares!

When there is a lull in the proceedings, a player may stand up and say "One". This means the game has commenced!

Someone else must then stand and say "two", followed by another player who says "three" etc.

The only rules are that no two people should stand at the same time (this incurs a three finger fine), and the last person to stand has to down their drink in one!

ESTD 1988

THE JUG
GAME

WORLD'S FINEST
ADULT
DRINKING

GAMES

THE JUG GAME

You need a large jug of beer for this game. The jug is passed round the table and each player drinks as little or as much as they wish. Tactics come into play as the jug is nearly empty. The rule is that the person who takes the PENULTIMATE drink has to buy the next jug.

Thus there comes a point when you have to decide whether you can finish what is left in the jug or whether you can risk leaving some, in which case if the next person empties it, the next jug is on you!

DRINKING GAMES COMPENDIUM

FINE INGREDIENTS AND A LOT OF HARD WORK

TRADE   MARK

· KILLER DARTS ·

GAME - JEU - GIUOCO

DRINKING GAMES COMPENDIUM

· KILLER DARTS ·

EQUIPMENT: A DARTS BOARD

Players take it in turns to throw a dart with their left hand to determine their number. Any player missing the board at this early stage should be severely penalised.

The aim is to try and become a "killer" by throwing your number five times. (Doubles and triples count as two and three throws.) Once you have become a killer you can try and hit other people's numbers and try and knock down their score. Every time you decrease someone's score by one, they have to pay a drinking fine. If someone is knocked down to minus one, they are out of the game. If you hit your own number while you are a killer then you lose one also - and have to throw your number again before you can regain killer status.

WORLD'S FINEST

ONLY THE FINEST INGREDIENTS ARE USED TO PRODUCE A PERFECT GAME

ESTD 1988

Knee Trembler

Diplome D'honneur

DRINKING GAME

PRIZE WINNER IN PARIS 1875, AMSTERDAM 1911, MUNICH 1921, SCUNTHORPE 1971

Knee Trembler

Place a large filled glass about ten feet away. Players take it in turns to drop five coins into the glass, all in one go.

The catch is that the coins must be held between your thighs. Players must still be able to walk and aim at the target. The result is a variety of very strange and amusing contortions! All the coins must go in in one go; if any "escape" then that go is invalid.

The last player to succeed has to drink what is in the glass.

EXPORT

**MANUFACTURED BY THE
PURVEYORS OF FINE ADULT DRINKING GAMES**

Liar Dice

The first player rolls all five dice, making sure that the others cannot see what he has thrown. When he declares what is being passed to the next player, this may or may not be the truth! The next player can either challenge this or accept. If he accepts, the second player then has to throw any number of the five dice again, telling the others how many he has thrown. He then declares what he is passing on, his score being HIGHER than the one he received.

SCORING: in ascending order of importance -

Five of a kind,

Four of a kind,

Full house (three of a kind and two of another),

Three of a kind,

Two pairs,

A Pair.

Higher numbers beat lower numbers, so three fives beat three ones. When a player CHALLENGES a throw, all five dice are revealed and the loser of the challenge has to pay a drinking forfeit before restarting the game with all five dice.

ESTD 1988

STRONG

Matchbox Game

PREMIUM

GOLD MEDAL

PARIS 1932

Matchbox Game

EQUIPMENT: A MATCHBOX

Players sit round a table, each with a drink. Everyone must take it in turn to throw a matchbox over their drink and onto the table. If the matchbox lands on its side, then a two finger fine is awarded to the next player; if on its end, a four finger fine is awarded to the next player, and if it lands flat nothing is passed on. The next player then throws and either passes on a new fine or, if the box lands flat, then they have to pay the fine passed on to them. Thus fines are accumulated and only when a player scores nothing does he have to drink.

If the matchbox lands in a drink then the thrower has to drink that drink and, if it belonged to someone else, buy them another one. Players missing the table completely are very sad people and should be dealt with gently but firmly.

TRADE MARK

THE
NAME
GAME

PREMIUM GAME

THE
NAME GAME

A NAME GAME REQUIRING A RAPID RESPONSE!

Players sit in a circle and someone starts by asking a question to which everyone must respond in turn. Each player must respond with a two word answer, which begins with the initials of their name. Thus if the question is "What is your favourite food?", Belinda Snodgrass might reply "boiled sweets" and Monty Cartwright might say "mouldy cheese".

A strict FIVE SECOND rule must be applied. Players failing to give an answer within the time limit or giving an answer deemed by the group to be substandard, should pay a minor drinking forfeit.

FINEST GAMES

OBSTACLE RACE

Hugh Jones

OBSTACLE RACE

EQUIPMENT: A DICE

The obstacles are made up of a line of four drinks, preferably varied.

The first player starts by rolling a dice. They must then decide whether their next throw will be higher or lower. If they guess correctly, they can then move past the first drink. The sequence must go alternatively, higher, lower, higher, lower so if they originally threw higher, they cannot move on past the second glass until they throw a lower number. Every time they fail, they must drink three fingers from the glass which is proving to be the obstacle.

Once a player has safely negotiated all obstacles, the glasses are replenished and the second player takes up the challenge.

TRADEMARK

ODDS ON
FAVOURITE

5·6%

DONCASTER
NEWMARKET
ASCOT
EPSOM
AINTREE

ODDS ON FAVOURITE

EQUIPMENT: A PACK OF CARDS

Each player is dealt a card which they immediately place on their forehead without looking at it.

Players now take turns to bet on whether their card is the highest one. (If you can see the other cards are an ace, an two and a three you would be tempted to bid quite high - say 4 fingers). The cards are revealed and the losers have to drink whatever the winner bid (in this case 4 fingers) plus their own individual bids.

Beware! Reckless bidding will result in a lot of drinking.

THE FINEST GAMES IN THE WORLD

THE FINEST GAMES IN THE WORLD

ONLY THE FINEST INGREDIENTS

ESTABLISHED IN NINETEEN HUNDRED AND EIGHTY-EIGHT

PIED PIPER

PIED PIPER

Each player needs a rat! This is a bottle top with a hole punched through it and a piece of string threaded through and knotted. Players place their rats in a pile in the centre of the table but keep hold of their tails.

A "rat catcher" is appointed and holds a bowl or large cup downwards at the edge of the table. He counts down "3, 2, 1, GO!" at which point he tries to catch as many rats as possible in the centre of the table while everyone else tries to pull their rat to safety.

Players are penalised:

- if their rat is caught (two finger drinking fine and disqualification from the game)

- if they snatch their rat away too early (drink four fingers but stay in the game).

The catcher is fined if he fails to catch any rats (two fingers). This game can get rather boisterous!

PUB GOLF

A SERIOUS DRINKING GAME FOR GOLF FANS!

For this Pro-Am tournament, players organise themselves into pairs, the Professional player is the pint drinker and the Amateur can either drink shorts or halves. Teams visit nine bars which represent the nine holes of the course. Each "hole" is par 3. In other words, each drink should be swallowed in three swigs to be "on par".

Scores are combined so that if the Pro drinks their pint in 4 swigs (ie. one over par), the Amateur needs to finish theirs in 2 to achieve Par for the hole. If the Pro player downs their drink in one, there is no need to combine scores, the Amateur player need not drink for that hole and the team can simply claim a hole-in-one. Each trip to the toilet costs one shot, falling over on the course costs two, "dropping your clubs" or undue spillage risks disqualification. Rules can be adapted to suit the drinking capacity of the players.

PUCKER AND SUCK

MANUFACTURED WITH IMMENSE PRIDE

TRADE MARK

ESTD 1988

PUCKER & SUCK

EQUIPMENT: A CREDIT CARD

A much more interesting variation of that children's game where you have to pass a matchbox between your knees or an orange under your chin.

In this version, players have to pass a credit card round in a ring using only their mouths and the power of suction. The first person places the card flat against their lips and sucks! The next person places their lips against the other side and they must suck whilst the first person blows. It's a game to get intimate with!

Fines are imposed if the card is dropped or if anyone cheats by using a different part of their body.

This game is improved by playing in mixed company.

SERGEANT MAJOR GENERAL

OBJECTIVE: TO AVOID THE DUNCE'S CHAIR!

Players are assigned ranks according to their position around the table: the first is a General, the player to their right is a Major, the next a Sergeant, then "one", "two", "three" and so on. The last player is labelled "Dunce". The General starts by standing, saying "General" and then somebody else's rank or number. If they say "General, Four" for example, it is now four's turn to stand, say their number and pass it on to somebody else. The only rule is that you may not send it back to the person who has just passed it to you or to the person either side of you. If a player does this, stands at the wrong time or hesitates, they have to pay a drinking forfeit and they become the DUNCE. They take the DUNCE'S seat and everyone in between has to adjust position accordingly, so acquiring new ranks and numbers.

TRADE MARK

SING SONG

A PREMIUM GAME
PLAY IN
MODERATION

SING SONG

The MC chooses a subject or colour: rain, blue, trains etc. Play goes round the table as each player sings a snippet from a song which contains a reference to that object or colour.

Thus if "Blue" is chosen, suitable offerings would be: "Blue Suede Shoes", "Don't It Make Your Brown Eyes Blue", "Blue Moon" etc.

If a player sings a song already selected, fails to come up with anything or simply sings appallingly then they must pay a hefty drinking fine.

THE LONDON CLASSIC

"DRINKING GAME"

SLAM

estd 1988

SLAM

NEEDED: PACK OF PLAYING CARDS

AIM: TO GET FOUR OF A KIND AND SLAM!

Prepare the deck of cards using four cards of a kind for each player. Shuffle this thoroughly and place a number of small objects (pennies, matches) in the centre of the table. There should be one less than the number of players. Deal the pack so each player has four mixed cards. Players examine their cards and, at a given signal, everyone pushes a card they do not want (face-down) to the player on their left. Everyone looks at their new card and decides whether to pass it on or exchange it for one from their hand. This continues until someone gets four of a kind. This player should then SLAM their hand down and quickly grab one of the objects. Everybody else follows suit, leaving someone without an object. This person has to drink a slammer (or other drink) before rejoining the game.

Drinking Game

SLAP ◆ CLAP

TRADE MARK

PLAY AT ROOM TEMPERATURE

SLAP · CLAP

OBJECTIVE: TO CALL OUT NAMES WHILST KEEPING IN TIME!

Players sit in a circle and start up a clapping rhythm by:

(1) SLAPPING their thighs with both hands, then

(2) CLAPPING their hands together and then

(3,4) CLICKING fingers on each hand in turn.

Practice until everyone is keeping the same rhythm!

Player one starts by saying "Names of", (slap, clap) "famous", (slap, clap) and then he or she must pick a category (beaches, types of car etc.) Each player follows in turn with a suitable word or name. The most important rule is that players can only speak on the finger-clicks, so the chosen word must be spread over two syllables to fit the rhythm. ("Bondi-Beach" or Toy-ota" for example). Anyone who hesitates, breaks the rhythm or who calls out a ridiculously inappropriate word has to take a drink. Categories can be as broad - or as limited - as you dare.

AN ADULT

SINCE 1988

SPOOF

PREMIUM

DRINKING GAME

SPOOF

EQUIPMENT: THREE COINS FOR EACH PLAYER. A KNOCKOUT GAMBLING GAME!

All players put their hands under the table and place 3, 2, 1, or indeed, none of the coins into one of their hands. This hand is then held closed over the table as players take turns to guess the TOTAL number of coins held in all the hands. Players should take turns in making first guess. Once all guesses have been made, everybody opens their hands and all the coins are counted. The person who has guessed correctly can retire safely to watch the next round. Everybody else has to take a drink. Whoever is left in at the end is the loser and has to undertake a major forfeit.

SPOON

ESTABLISHED ✕ NINETEEN TEN

THE CROSSED SPOONS ARE
A TRADEMARK OF THE SPOON BREWING CO.

GAME

SPOON GAME MANUFACTURERS SINCE THE DAY BEFORE YESTERDAY

SPOON GAME

Two players are pitted against each other, one of whom should be new to the game.

Players sit opposite each other, each with a tablespoon held between their teeth. Each must, in turn, bend forward and allow the other to hit them on the back of the head with the spoon. As the spoon is only held in their mouth, this should not really hurt. Play continues until a player drops out.

The trick is that someone stands behind the victim with a larger spoon or ladle. When the victim bends forward, they are dealt a hefty blow by the ladle holder. They obviously assume it is the other player and try to get their own back which only leads to further suffering and increasing frustration. It is hilarious for all onlookers but ultimately you will have to put the victim out of their misery!

STICKY TOFFEE PUDDING

OBJECTIVE: TO KEEP YOUR TEETH HIDDEN!

Everyone chooses one of the following desserts: Bread and Butter Pudding, Poached Pears in White Wine, Mississippi Mud Pie, Maple Syrup Tart, Creme Caramel Surprise, Blackberry Brulee, Gooseberry Fool, Zabaglione, Caramelised Peaches, Chocolate Profiteroles.

The first player calls out their pudding name followed by another player's. That player must call out their pudding name followed by another's and so on. The only snag is, that players must talk WITHOUT showing their TEETH.

Any glimpse of tooth enamel, no matter how fleeting, is punished with a drinking forfeit. Laughing is, of course, the most grievous of misdemeanours and should gigglers fail to cover their mouths in time, they should be penalised with a major drinking forfeit. Similarly, players must take care that their speech is intelligible as incoherent speech also attracts a forfeit.

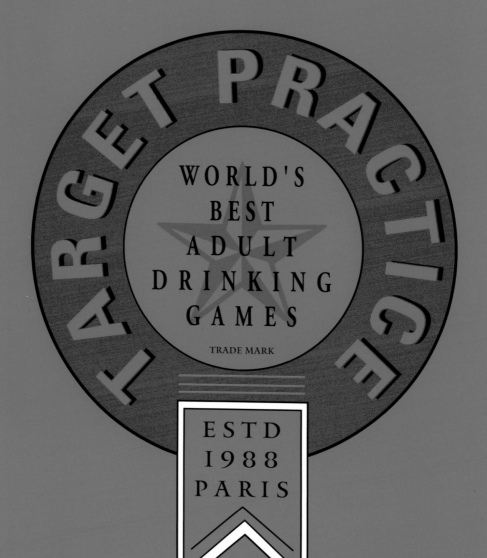

TARGET PRACTICE

EQUIPMENT: A COIN

Players sit round a table with their drinks placed all together in the centre. Right in the very middle of the table is placed a large empty glass.

Players take turns to bounce a coin off the table and into another person's drink. Whoever owns the drink which is "coined" has to drink four fingers.

If a player succeeds in bouncing the coin into their own drink then they have to drink the whole glass; likewise if they manage to bounce the coin right off the table.

If the coin lands in the centre glass then the whole company has to drink.

THINK AS YOU DRINK

OBJECTIVE: TO THINK QUICKLY OF FAMOUS NAMES!

Player one starts by calling out a famous person's name - say "Marc Bolan". Player two must follow by calling out a famous person whose first name starts with the letter of the last person's surname. Thus, "Bill Clinton" could follow, then "Cyril Regis", and so on.

Whilst a player is thinking of a name to call out, he must drink his drink. Whilst this is happening, other players are at liberty to call out appropriate names thereby disqualifying them. So if someone calls out "Bill Clinton" while you are still drinking …and thinking…that is a name you cannot use! Players should endeavour to call out as many names as possible so that the drinker is forced to continue drinking until they come up with something original.

If someone calls out a name where both initials are the same - say Marilyn Monroe - then the order of play is reversed.

The
Truth Game

estd 1988
Adult Drinking Game

The Truth Game

This needs to be played amongst close friends and intimates! Player one starts by declaring "I have never been... (somewhere)" or alternatively, "I have never done... (something)". It could be anything - from visiting a massage parlour to reading "Hello!" magazine.

Any player who HAS done this thing has to drink one finger. Any player who denies the deed but was spotted doing it by someone else, has to drink two fingers. Any player who actually boasts that they have done a particular deed, but who is believed to be lying, has the most severe penalty of all and has to drink four fingers.

The MC must exert strict control over this game or it may get violent!

ESTD 1988

UNSTUCK

STRONG

PRIZE WINNERS AT THE PARIS EXHIBITION OF BEER
IN 1932. DUSSELDORF 1934. ADELAIDE 1949.

UNSTUCK

This game works as a hoax, so the group needs to include a "victim" - someone who has never played it before.

Tell the victim that a coin is going to be "stuck" to their forehead. They then have to hit themselves on the back of the head, to see how many hits it will take to dislodge the coin. Give a demonstration: it is a good idea to lick the coin before placing it on your forehead. After a few gentle knocks, the coin will come off.

It looks simple. When your victim is ready, move to place the coin on their forehead but don't really put it there - just push firmly. They will believe the coin is there and so bash themselves on the back of the head repeatedly, but to no avail. It is up to you to decide when to put the poor player out of their misery.

WIBBLY WOBBLY

EQUIPMENT: TWO BROOM HANDLES OR POLES

Players line up in two teams, each person holding a full drink. On the word "Go!", the first player must down their drink and run over to the broom handle. They have to place one end of the stick against their forehead (leaving the other on the floor) and run round it ten times.

The really tricky bit is running back to your team mates in a straight line afterwards to try and tag the next member!

The winning team is the one which finishes first. Warning: possible side effects include headaches and nausea.

WARNING

We recommend that you play these games with non-alcoholic beverages. However, please read and follow these important instructions and warnings prior to playing any of the following drinking games. Failure to follow these instructions and warnings may result in serious injury or death.

- These drinking games are for adults age 21 and over only.

- Do not operate an automobile if you drink alcoholic beverages while playing any of these drinking games.

- No-one who must operate an automobile within the next 12 hours should play any drinking game with alcoholic beverages.

- Use plastic bottles or cups or cans only. No glass should be used while playing any drinking game.

- Stop if you feel dizzy or sick while playing.

- Do not drink more alcoholic beverages than the legal limit while playing any drinking game.

- Do not play these drinking games where it is against local rules or laws, such as campus rules at university.

- In no case should anyone who has had alcoholic beverages while playing any drinking game drive an automobile until at least 12 hours after playing.

- Consult any label of medication you are taking for limitations of alcohol intake prior to playing any drinking game.

- According to the Surgeon General, women should not drink alcoholic beverages during pregnancy because of the risk of birth defects.

- Consumption of alcoholic beverages impairs your ability to drive a car or operate machinery, and may cause health problems.

- We strongly recommend alternatives to drinking forfeits are used to moderate alcohol intake.